CW01177590

Other Books Written by Karolyn Evans Jennings

Phases of Love, 1992), KEE & Associates
Rhyme and Jive, 1993, KEE & Associates
The Artist at Work, 1993, KEE & Associates
KEE & Associates Publishing and Printing
19381 Gable Street, Detroit, MI 48234

From Me to You, 2019
Xlibris Publications

Black Queens Speak, 2021
iUniverse Publications

Yesterday's Memories Today's Realities, 2023
Xlibris Publications

SONGS OF PRAISE

God is Good All the Time

KAROLYN E. JENNINGS

WESTBOW
PRESS®
A DIVISION OF THOMAS NELSON
& ZONDERVAN

Copyright © 2024 Karolyn E. Jennings.

All rights reserved. No part of this book may be used or reproduced by any means, graphic, electronic, or mechanical, including photocopying, recording, taping or by any information storage retrieval system without the written permission of the author except in the case of brief quotations embodied in critical articles and reviews.

This book is a work of non-fiction. Unless otherwise noted, the author and the publisher make no explicit guarantees as to the accuracy of the information contained in this book and in some cases, names of people and places have been altered to protect their privacy.

WestBow Press books may be ordered through booksellers or by contacting:

WestBow Press
A Division of Thomas Nelson & Zondervan
1663 Liberty Drive
Bloomington, IN 47403
www.westbowpress.com
844-714-3454

Because of the dynamic nature of the Internet, any web addresses or links contained in this book may have changed since publication and may no longer be valid. The views expressed in this work are solely those of the author and do not necessarily reflect the views of the publisher, and the publisher hereby disclaims any responsibility for them.

Any people depicted in stock imagery provided by Getty Images are models, and such images are being used for illustrative purposes only. Certain stock imagery © Getty Images.

Scripture quotations) are taken from the King James Version, public domain.

ISBN: 979-8-3850-3358-4 (sc)
ISBN: 979-8-3850-3359-1 (e)

Library of Congress Control Number: 2024919378

Print information available on the last page.

WestBow Press rev. date: 09/11/2024

MY BLESSINGS

Thanks to God for my inspiration and gifts and my sisters.

To my son Ebon, explore and use all your God given talents and travel as far as you can on the road of life.

To my niece Tamika, God is Good All the Time and His Miracles are wonders to behold. You are living proof of that.

To my actress niece, RuVonna, God loves you and so do I, I know you will work hard to bring all your talents and dreams to reality.

To Lexi, I only expect exceptional discoveries in your future.

To my grand- nieces and grand-nephews and grandchildren, you are all God's gifts to me and one day you will realize that He has great plans for your lives.

Ernest, I thank God for every day He gave you to me, You always made my heart sing!

GOD IS GOOD
(All the Time)

God is good all the time
Those were the words she said
God is good all the time
She even spoke them
On her death bed.
Unbelievable Faith, Undeniable Faith
Faith the size of a mustard seed that had grown into a Mount Everest
Strong Faith, Doubtless Faith, Everlasting Faith,
That was the kind of Faith Tanina had.

God is good all the time
Those were the words she said
God is good all the time
Is the Legacy she left her family.

In loving memory of Tanina L. Edwards,
My aunt and lifelong friend.

*This book is dedicated to
All who believe Prayer makes the
Impossible Possible*

CONTENTS

LET ME TELL YOU ABOUT JESUS

Let Me Tell You About Jesus 1
Celebrate The Living Christ 2
Stars 3
Love Finds A Way 4
Jesus Kept Me 5
I Am 6
People In Love 7
Your Love's The Same As When The Day Began 8
Who I Am 9

JESUS KEEPS ME

Resting 13
Sometimes I Wonder 14
To A Better Day 15
Today 16
He Never Promised 17
When I Call On Jesus 18
A Special Love 19

JESUS MY SAVIOR MY FRIEND

Only You 22
Let Me Learn 23
Jesus' Love Remains The Same 24
Sunday Morning 25
In Tune 26
Walking With Jesus 27
Whenever I See Stars 28

AT THE CROSSROADS OF LIFE

If You But Seek Him	31
Reach Out	32
Trust In The Lord	33
Gently Stroking	34
Mountains.	35
Ribbon Of Discord	36
You Have Got To Come Through Jesus	37
Forgetfulness	38
Just Say The Word	39
Lost/Sinking	40
Touch Me Lord	41

GOD'S HOUSE

Welcome To My Church House	45
Fan The Flame	46

MY MIDNIGHT RIDER

Midnight	49
My Midnight Rider	50
I Have Got A Friend	51
You Have Made My Life A Lamp To Shine	52

PRAYER MAKES THE IMPOSSIBLE POSSIBLE

Distance	55
One Mother's Prayer	56
Wishing You Well	57
A Prayer (Lord Here I Am Looking Up)	57
I Pray Each Night Upon My Knees.	58
Sometimes Lord	59

HEAVEN BOUND

I'm Going Home Today 97
Homeward Bound 98
I Heard Jesus Call 98
Remember 99
Christian Women 100
Move Up Just A Little Bit Higher 101
That Day Not So Far Away 102
A Homegoing Song 103
When You Stand In Front Of God 104

JESUS SAVED ME

Walking With Jesus 107
Family And Friend Day 108
Come Unto Me 109
Lord Linger Near 110
Jesus Set Me Free 111

There Must Be An Answer 60
When In Doubt 61
When It Is Your Turn 62
All Shall Praise His Name 63

I KNOW THAT GOD SAVED ME

Smiles 67
He Is So Good 67
Your Light 68
Whispering In The Wind 69
Hallelujah, Jesus Set Me Free 71
The Castle 73
I Know That God Saved Me 74
Jesus Cares (Today His Love Is The Only Way) 75
I Found Jesus 76
Just A Little Faith ....
The Future ....

GOD WILL NEVER LET YOU FALL

God Will Never Let You Fall ....
Jesus Power ....
Look Up ....
A Faithful Prayer ....
Mighty Is The Lord ....
Marvel ....
Carry On In The Name Of The Lord ....
You Will Find All You Need In Me ....
And Why Should I Be Afraid ....
The Devil Is Working Overtime ....

Psalm 92: 1
It is a good thing to give thanks unto the Lord, and to sing praises unto thy name, O most high.

LET ME TELL YOU ABOUT JESUS

O Lord, how great are thy works! and thy thoughts are very deep.

PSALM 92:5

LET ME TELL YOU ABOUT JESUS

Let me tell you about Jesus
He is a mighty good friend
When you give your best to Him,
He will give the same in return.

If you just take one step
The Lord will give you two
When you give your best to Him,
He will make your life brand new.

Let me tell you what He has done for me
He kept His promises true.
When He hears my cry,
He answered always, right on time.

Give your best to Jesus
Give Him your all and all
Give the most that you can give,
His love will make you strong.

Chorus:
Trust in Him who loves you
Trust in Him who cares
Give the Lord the best you can give
His love will make you strong.

CELEBRATE THE LIVING CHRIST

There are questions being asked around the world.

They are asking does Christ really live,
They are asking when He will come again.
There are questions being asked among the people
Can Christ be my refuge and my strength,
Can Christ arrest my pain and fear,
Can Christ River flood my valley?

They are asking if the Christ can change your life?

There are questions being asked among the people
About the saving grace of Jesus Christ
Wandering lost souls, saved and faithful souls.
The weak, the meek and the pure in heart.
They are all asking questions about my Christ.
The young, the old and those saved by grace,
The poor, the rich and those full of faith.

I say,
Celebrate the Living Christ
It's a celebration!
Celebrate the Living Christ
It's a celebration!

STARS

Stars spread out across God's heaven
Winking down at you and me
Oh, to be a star so bright
And light a path so man can see.

Stars encircle God's great earth
Stars alone that He created.
He hung them in a sky of black
To be night lights for you and me.

LOVE FINDS A WAY

Love finds a way when all else has failed.
Love finds a way when we no longer seek it.
Love seeps into the empty spaces,
And lets our old memories flow.

Love travels in our bloodstream
The ones we thought were cold
Love rests upon our hearts,
The heart we thought was broken.

Love hovers around our bodies
This love, we no longer feel.
Love softens the hard knocks in life
And replaces our every hurt.

Love will open the doors to hearts
That grief has tried to close.
Love can go where no man has ever gone before.
Love finds a way, if we remember that Jesus loves us.

JESUS KEPT ME

As I travel down life's long road
I know He is constantly by me side.
I know my prayers He will answer
And answer right on time.

The road is so long and weary
It twists and turns constantly
I know when I get to the bend,
You will be there to walk with me.

Jesus kept me,
Jesus kept me,
Every step of the way,
Jesus kept me.

I AM

I am the star of Egypt
I shine brightly for all to see.
I am the light when darkness falls,
I am the peacemaker when trouble calls.
I am water when you thirst,
I am food when you hunger.
I am eyes when you cannot see,
I am ears when you don't want to hear.
I am a shoulder, when you need to lean,
I am a staff, when you cannot stand.
I am a guide, when you don't know the way,
I am your compass when you can't read the stars.
I am the voice that shatters all barriers,
That may try to block your way.
I am the only one with a master plan,
I am the star of Egypt.

PEOPLE IN LOVE

People in love the world around
Enduring love that knows no bounds.
Faithful love beyond compare
Enriching love, the need to share.

Binding love that's so secure
Wanting love that keeps it pure.
Loving hearts endowed with power
Peaceful love that doesn't turn sour.

People in love the world around
Joyful love so warm and sweet
Hopeful love that can't be beat.

YOUR LOVE'S THE SAME AS WHEN THE DAY BEGAN

Oh Lord my God, deep in my heart you abide
Oh Lord my God, all my needs You supply
You never change, Unlike the seasons rearranged
You never lie, your love as You promised in abundant supply.

I love You Lord, With You in my life I am strong
I love You Lord, With You I am never alone
You never change, Your love remains the same
You never lie, in my heart You will always abide.

I love the Lord
He means the world to me,
I love you Lord
You fulfill all my needs.
You never lie,
You love in abundant supply.
You never change,
Your love remains the same.

And when I wake
At the break of day
Your love's the same as yesterday.

And when I lay down
to sleep at night
Your love's the same as when the day began.

WHO I AM

I am happy because I know who I am
I do not worry about the people that do not know me,
Because I know for myself, just who I am.

I am happy because I know God loves me
I do not worry about people that do not love me.
Because I know for myself that God loves me.

I can love my brothers and sisters everywhere
My love overflows wherever I go,
Because God loves me, and I know who I am.

JESUS KEEPS ME

The Lord is my shepherd, I shall not want.
―――――――
PSALM 23:1

RESTING

Kenny is resting with the angels. In a quiet, peaceful place.
In a valley filled with wonder, and Glory from on high,
The moment he crossed that serene river,
He met Jesus with a glorious cry.
No more mountains, no more valleys, will he ever have to cross,
We are rejoicing in the fact that his soul was never lost.
Lost from the face of Jesus, away from His saving grace,
Yes, Kenny is resting with the angels, in a quiet, peaceful place.
I love you and I will miss you and as long as I remember your smile,
You will always live in my heart.

Your Loving Sister

SOMETIMES I WONDER

Sometimes I wonder
Just where I would be
If Jesus had not come to set me free.

I wonder if I would be
The person I am
Or be going down the wrong pathway.

Sometimes I wonder
Just what God has planned for me,
Since He has been in my life
It's so loving and carefree.

My worries are gone
My problems are few
Life is wonderful
I feel brand new.

Sometimes I wonder
Just where I would be,
If Jesus had not come to set me free.

He died on the cross so that I can see,
Someday the kingdom He is preparing for me.

TO A BETTER DAY

I am on my way to the promised land
Will you go with me as I journey there
I know a better day is coming soon
Where the sun will always shine,
The birds will sing songs all day,
Nights will shine bright with glorious light,
The trees and flowers will forever bloom,
And no one will know the meaning of gloom.

Chorus:
The mountains that rise so majestically
Above the old world below
Will house the new kingdom coming
Are you going with me, or do I travel alone?

TODAY

I woke up this morning
Thanked God for this brand-new day
Because without the Lord
This day would have never come.

I heard the birds singing
And the crickets humming
Singing praises in the morning
For the day that had just begun.

At twilight I said my prayers
Thanking God for this brand-new day
I had made it through
And rising from my knees, I thought

About the morning sounds I had heard
The sounds of birds and crickets
And now at twilight they were humming,
The song of praise I had heard that morning.

HE NEVER PROMISED

Jesus never promised you a rose garden
Or great happiness every day
He did not say the road would be easy
Without crossroads, twists and turns.

The roses die in autumn
To bloom again next spring
And the sun does shine everyday
But not enough to take away all the pain.

But Jesus did promise, life everlasting
If you believed in Him
And the riches of His Father's kingdom
If you would just follow Him.

He promised to prepare a place for you and me,
So, we could forever dwell,
Close by His side in His heavenly mansion
Without a worry or a care.

WHEN I CALL ON JESUS

When I call on Jesus
I know He will answer prayer
For if I did not believe in Him
I would doubt His loving care.

I call on You, Jesus
I do not know what else to do
For you promised love everlasting
Peace of mind and miracles unsurpassed.

I will always believe in You, Jesus
Your love so permanent and true
I would be so lost Lord
If I did not have faith in you.

You have always been my friend
By my side through thick and thin
Faith allows me to win
I realized it in the end.

I know You know what is best
But is my faith always to test?
I know deep in my heart
Justice You earnestly impart.

A SPECIAL LOVE

There is a special love indeed
I hold it close to my heart.
And if I treasure it dearly,
It will never depart.

There is a special love indeed
The love of Jesus Christ.
And if I love and believe in Him
His love I will never need to part.

JESUS MY SAVIOR MY FRIEND

A friend loveth at all times, and a brother is born of adversity.
PROVERBS 17:17

ONLY YOU

Only You,
Know the real me.
Only You,
Know how I really feel.
Only You,
Can see deep down in my soul.

Down where no one else can see
You know the secrets of the deep.
You know the secrets
That fall down in the cracks and crevices of my soul.

Only You,
Know the secrets that I cannot hide.

"OH"

The sun was shining
"Oh" so bright, this morning when I arose
I felt the love of God
"Oh' such light, as I arose to greet the dawn.
I felt my burdens lifted
"Oh" what weight, in the glorious light of day.
The prayer I said last night
"Oh" what a prayer, I knew would be heard by morn.
I know Jesus hears us all
"Oh" what and ear, no matter when we call.

LET ME LEARN

Let me learn to be patient,
Let me learn to hold my peace,
Let me learn to love my brother and my sister too,
As I live each day strong and true.

You know tomorrow, is not promised
It is not given for granted, it is not sure
That it is coming for you or for me.

I know about temptation, it sometimes gets in the way
It seems to push and pull me, the worldly way
Give me strength and power to overcome each day.

Chorus:
We must learn
We must learn
To live one day at a time,
Teach me Lord, teach me Lord,
To wait patiently.

JESUS' LOVE REMAINS THE SAME

A strong wind has the strength
To knock you down on your knees
A strong wind has the power
To bend you to its will
The weather changes every day, yet it doesn't change a thing
Because Jesus love remains the same.

The storms of life can shake
The foundations of your faith
Make you feel so hurt and alone
Shake you up and turn you around.
But you can face your troubles and trials
Because Jesus love remains the same.

The storms of life will toss you
Like the raging waves in the sea
Solid ground becomes sinking sand
Because you forgot one thing
The weather changes every day, yet it doesn't change a thing
Because Jesus love remains the same.

I do not know what tomorrow's going to bring
It may be sunshine, it might even be rain
The weather changes every day, but it doesn't change a thing
Because Jesus love remains the same.

SUNDAY MORNING

Jesus came to me one Sunday
Clapping in my hands
I have been clapping ever since
Jesus came to me one Sunday.

Stomping in my feet
I have been stomping my feet ever since
Jesus came to me one Sunday.

Shouting in my mouth
I have been shouting ever since
Jesus came to me one Sunday.

Singing in my soul
I have been singing ever since
Jesus came to me one Sunday.

Has the Holy Ghost touched you
And changed your life?
Has the Holy ghost touched you?
I have been changed
You have got to live for Jesus every day.

Lead:	*Jesus came into my life*
Chorus:	*I have been changed*
Lead:	*I am living for Jesus every day*
	Yes, I am clapping, shouting, and singing His praise
Chorus:	*Ooh I am living, living, living for Jesus*

IN TUNE

There is a humming way down in my soul
The words I hear are so sweet and clear
There is a humming in my soul.

There is a melody playing in my soul
The chords I hear flow strong and clear
There is a melody playing in my soul

I have a song to sing from my soul
The words I song are so warm and free
I have a song to sing from my soul.

The words to my song are alive
The words are alive because my Christ is too,
And they originate way down in my soul.

WALKING WITH JESUS

My shoes are worn
My clothes are not new
But my faith in Jesus
Will see me through.
I have come this far
I cannot turn around
I know He will answer
Me right on time.

I have been walking with Jesus
All of my life
He is always by my side
Whether I am wrong or I am right.
My faith keeps me near
I know He will hear
Whenever I call,
Whenever I call.

WHENEVER I SEE STARS

Whenever I see stars
        Shining so high in the sky
        So brightly lit for the world to see.
I think of love
        Waiting to burst
        Into millions of particles and expand.

Far beyond the known horizons
        Of the universe.
Love exceeds all bounds
Eludes all restrictions
Restricts, where illusions proceed
Love transcends beyond the universe.

Unrestricted, unleashed love
        Transforms unfeeling into feeling
Transforms unreal into real
Makes the knowledge of love accessible,
        To all who care to try.

AT THE CROSSROADS OF LIFE

*For thou art my rock and my fortress;
therefore, for thy name's sake
lead me and guide me.*

PSALMS 31:3

IF YOU BUT SEEK HIM

They told me about Jesus
How He could fill my life
They told me about the miracles
That He performs out right.
They told me I could find Him
If I just lifted my voice.

They told me He answers prayer,
That He would see me through
The many trials and tribulations,
That life will put me through
And if I will remove me first
The blessings will flow anew.

All the talk about Jesus
And the way He would fill my life
With love and happiness
And appease the empty spaces,
Made me want to seek Him
But I just did not know where.

Chorus:

If you but seek Him	*If you but seek Him*
You will find Him	*He will find you*
For His love is everywhere	*For He knows just what you need*
If you but seek Him	*If you but seek Him*
You will find Him	*He will find you*
His spirit is always there.	*For His love will see you through*

REACH OUT

*If you would just reach out and touch someone
and maybe change their day.
Just reach out and take someone's hand
and let them know you care.
Wipe away a tear of sorrow with tender loving kindness.
A kiss will take away the pain and leave a tiny reminder.*

*Show concern when someone's troubled
and provide a listening ear.
Gently grip a tired shoulder that troubles
often bend.
Just reach out a little every day,
and it will change your life.*

*For the very time you feel unloved,
A touch will change your day.*

TRUST IN THE LORD

I have got to trust in the Lord everyday
Without Him to guide me I may lose my way
He gives me hope for a better tomorrow
He wipes away my tears and eases my sorrow
With Him my way is bright and new
Without Him I do not know what I would do.

Chorus

He is my hope, and He is my way
He is my strength for a better day
Without Him I do not know what I would do
Without Him I do not know what I could do.

GENTLY STROKING

So peaceful and calm
Silent waves wash
        Up the sandy beach
Gently stroking, gently stroking.

Relaxing thoughts once
Full of turmoil with stormy
        Solutions
Gently stroking, gently stroking.

Problems seem to dissolve
Only loved ones are missed
        But still loved
Gently stroking, gently stroking.

Wade in the water
It is so peaceful there
        And God is constantly
Gently stroking, gently stroking.

MOUNTAINS.

Mountains that rise to touch God's heaven
Meet a million stars along the way.
They look down upon God's mountains
And stretch themselves out to play.

Touch me if you can
Come up to meet me
I will be here waiting
If you care to try.

If you can't come play with me
I will spin circles above your head.

Don't get dizzy.

RIBBON OF DISCORD

There is a ribbon of discord
Running through my life tonight
It is not of my own making
However, it is one I can abide.

When you know you have been a good friend or family member
And have done everything in your power to always be right there
It is not a happy feeling
To know that your friend or relative never really cared.

To be pushed to the wayside
On the first momentous day
On the day of future tomorrow's
The day they will start to pay.

There is a ribbon of discord
Running through my life tonight
And in my heart, I know
God will make it alright.

YOU HAVE GOT TO COME THROUGH JESUS

Chorus
You have got to come through Jesus
It might as well be right now
He is standing there to let you in
He will not turn you back, if you are sincere.

Verse
I woke up this morning feeling so fine
I knew that my Jesus was walking by my side.
I had to go and spread (tell) the good news
And tell the world just what my Jesus would do.

I started walking down the street
My happy feet moved to a brand-new beat.
He is standing there to take your hand
If you are not ready - He will help you to stand.

You have got to come through Jesus
It might as well be right now. (Repeat)
He is standing there to take your hand
If you are not ready, He will help you to stand.

FORGETFULNESS

*Whenever I am in trouble
I call on my Jesus' name
To help me with my problems
I know He will prevail.*

*But when times are good
And blessings overflow
I seem sometimes to forget
That Jesus is still my blessing.*

*So, I must not forget Him
When times are good
For He might not hear me
When times are bad.*

JUST SAY THE WORD

Just say the word
And I will be all that you would have me to be.
Just say the word
And I will be what you want me to be.
You know I have worked hard all my life
Living with pain and mental strife
Surviving every day as best I can
Loving and respecting my fellow man.

Working to make a future plan
Giving to life the best I can
Teaching my child the rights from wrongs,
Praying every day, he will grow honest, tall and strong.

Calling on my Jesus both day and night
Knowing He will hear this one child's cry.
Trusting on His word is what I do
Loving Him has made my life brand new.

Just say the word
And I will be, all that you would have me to be
Just say the word, and I will be the best that I can be.

LOST/SINKING

When I was lost sinking in sin
You came along and would not let the devil win
I was mired in the sinking sand
Then You came along and gave me Your hand.
When I lay dying in a cold, cold bed
There was no hope by the standards of man
Dr. Jesus came into the room
Lifted my spirits and raised life anew.
Now I can say every day
There is no doubt, Jesus is the way
I just want to say, Thank you Lord for
Giving me back my life.
Thank you, Lord, for another day

TOUCH ME LORD

Touch me Lord today
And please do not forget
Me tonight.
I am so all alone
And I really need
A friend.

I know you have
The answer to all
My trials and tribulations.
So, touch me Lord
I pray
In my midnight of today.

GOD'S HOUSE

Behold I stand at the door and knock, if any man hear my voice, and open the door, I will come in to him, and will sup with him, and he with me.

REVELATION 3:20

WELCOME TO MY CHURCH HOUSE

Welcome to my Church house
The doors to the Church
Are always open wide.
I welcome you in the name of our Lord and Savior Jesus Christ,
And ***always*** I welcome you back.
My building is made of bricks and mortar,
I have wood and concrete floors,
I have bright lights so that you can see,
And benches upon which you may rest.
Sometimes my thermostat is set too high and makes you get too hot,
Sometimes the air runs too fast, and it can make you feel cool.
Every now and then I need dusting and cleaning, maybe even airing out,
But let us get down to basics because a building's not
    All that I am about.
You see, it is the *MINISTERS* as they preach and teach in the pulpit,
    About living the word in everyday life.
It is the *MINISTERS WIVES* as they walk with their husbands,
    In and out of the building.
It is the wisdom of the *MOTHERS* that sit and sing and shout,
    As they praise the Lord,
And the *DEACONS* that pray and sing and moan and direct
    Young and old alike.
Then there are my *TEACHERS* and *MUSICIANS* and *CHOIRS*
and *USHERS*
    And *PARENTS* and *YOUTHS*, that make it a *Church Home*
Of which I have chosen to describe just a few.
But everyone who is a MEMBER here welcomes you just as graciously.
My doors have been open for 76 ***Years*** and we pray for many, many more.

FAN THE FLAME

I may not be the usher,
Who greets you with a smile,
And shows you to your seat.
I may not be the deacon,
Who prays for your soul's salvation,
To the highest degree.

I may not be the lead singer
Singing Zion's songs that
Bring you standing to your feet.
I may not be the preacher,
Who petitions God Almighty,
To save your soul and bring you grace.

But I can fan the flames,
That Jesus started long ago,
The fire that burns eternally will forever glow.

I can fan the flame of Christ,
In all I do and say,
Because I know my God
Has already made a way.
I may not be as great as some,
I may not always be in front,
But in God's book we are all the same.

And I can fan the flame of
Christ every single day.

MY MIDNIGHT RIDER

*Thou lifted me up to the wind, then causes' me to ride upon it;
and dissolves my substances.*

JOB 30:22

MIDNIGHT

In the midnight hour Lord
When the world is standing still
I can hear your footfalls,
As they pass my windowsill.

I know you have and ear to hear,
A heart filled with compassion.
I know you will answer me,
I can feel it when I'm still.

There is a slight rushing,
I feel in my heart,
I know in my heart,
I know your blessings
In the midnight hour you impart.

MY MIDNIGHT RIDER

Jesus is my midnight rider
I felt Him riding by
He touched my head
He touched my heart
I felt Him move inside.

He went to all my troubled placed
Within my unsettled world
He told me it would be alright
And healed my wounded soul.

He made me see
How good things could be
If I just held to my belief.
Jesus is my Midnight Rider
He always brings R-E-L-I-E-F.

Chorus

His spirit is like a Fire Horse
Dancing and prancing deep in my soul
Waiting for the starting signal
To heal my troubled soul.

Already, all willing, all able
Dancing and prancing deep inside
To heal my troubled soul.

I HAVE GOT A FRIEND

I have got a friend, who is so dear
Every day of my life, that friend is near

He walks beside me, both day and night
No matter where I go, He keeps me in His sight.

I man lose sight of Him when I am
Down and out and troubled by the world.

But my friend never,
Ever loses sight of me.

YOU HAVE MADE MY LIFE A LAMP TO SHINE

Deliver me O' Lord to the light
Guide my feet I pray in the way that's right.
Touch my heart so that I may be,
The Christian, you taught me to be
You have made my life a lamp for me to shine.

Guide me O' Lord to a better day
Lift my burdens I pray and cast them away.
Feed my soul so that I may know,
The beauty of living for you
You have made my life a lamp for me to shine.

Touch my heart O' Lord in a special way
Help me, I pray to love my brother more each day.
Give me the strength to carry on,
As I live each day for you
You have made my life a lamp for me to shine.

Chorus:
He picked me up when I was down
Led me to the Light and now I'm found
Now I can give in return
What he has given me
You have made my life a lamp for me to shine.

PRAYER MAKES THE IMPOSSIBLE POSSIBLE

And Jesus said unto him, if thou canst believe, all things are possible to him that believeth.

MARK 9:23

DISTANCE

When I am burdened and heavy laden
And all is not peaceful within
My mind reminds me of the troubles,
Between me, my family and friends.

The distance that now separates us
And keeps us far apart
Because one of us is saying, "I'm hurting"
And the other does not seem to care.

We close our hearts to each other
Disrespect follows close at our heels,
Overlooking and ignoring each other's contribution
As if in this life none were ever made.

We smile and say the right words
As each word twists someone's heart
We now talk and do not look into the eyes,
That we looked into all our lives.

The eyes that stare unforgiving
Eyes angry and smoldering
Eyes wide with disbelief
Eyes that are cold and impersonal.

Now I'm burdened and heavy laden
And is not peaceful within.
I pray God will allow forgiveness and peace,
To come back to our lives again.

ONE MOTHER'S PRAYER

I am calling again Lord,
Asking you to watch over my child,
But not just my child
Every mother's child.

We can walk through life with them,
But we can't always walk with them,
the way you do.
We can teach them right from wrong,
But we can't make them do right.
We can teach them to make choices,
But we can't make their choices
for them.

When they are out in the streets, and
On their way to school, and in school
When they socialize with their friends
And are confronted by their enemies, when they
Feel the pressure of wrong pulling them,
Help them to do right.

When they are downhearted and disappointed,
Let them know we are here for them, and they can
Come to us anytime of the day and night.

Touch all the children and guide them through the day.

Watch my son and keep him safe, till I can hug him and say,
"I love you," one more time this day.

WISHING YOU WELL

Wishing you more than your share of God's blessings,
Wishing you more good things that life has to offer,
Wishing you well, God speed you along your way
I wish you well, I do wish you well.

A PRAYER
(Lord Here I Am Looking Up)

Lord here I am looking up,
From down on my knees
Asking you to please
Hear my prayer.

Lord, here I am looking up,
For an answer from above
I know you can and will
Answer my prayer.

Where would I go if I did not have you,
Where would I be if you did not see
The things the world has put on me.

You opened the doors so I could be
Close to you, so much closer to you.

I PRAY EACH NIGHT UPON MY KNEES.

I pray each night upon my knees,
That God will hear my plea.
I pray each night upon my knees,
The Lord will answer please.
I pray each night upon my knees,
That God who reigns above,
Will heed my call and not turn His head,
And touch my life instead.

I pray each night upon my knees,
That He will always stay close by.
I pray each night upon my knees the I will
be strong and keep the faith.
I pray each night upon my knees,
That the God who reigns above,
Will keep me in his glorious grace,
And lead me to His Heavenly Place.

SOMETIMES LORD
(Why Can't It Be Like I Want It To Be)

Ooh Lord
Sometimes Lord
Why can't it be like I
want it to be.

It might not be good for me,
But happy I will be,
It might not be in Your plans,
But it's still in Your hands.

It might not be what I need,
But I will be ooh so pleased.
If only for a little while
If only for the passing time.

Ooh Lord
Sometimes Lord
Why can't it be like I
want it to be.

THERE MUST BE AN ANSWER

There must be an answer somewhere,
But where do I start to look?

I can start by looking at myself,
The spiritual self and none other.

I can put aside all desire for material,
Satisfaction and selfish gain.

And strive to satisfy the spiritual self,
And work for God's glorious gain.

Once I can do this sincerely with all
My heart and soul and mind.

I know I can find an answer,
My answer will forever walk by my side.

WHEN IN DOUBT

Whenever you begin to doubt
What the power of Jesus is all about
Remember how He has blessed you in the past,
Remember all the good things He has given you,
Start to recall if you can,
Count the times when He did not answer your prayer,
And I know you cannot!
When in doubt, shout Hallelujah, Jesus is mine!

When dark clouds are hovering over
And the sun refuses to shine,
Just remember what I told you about King Jesus,
He is a friend of mine.
When the good in life seems to pass you by
And you begin to wonder why?
Look to the One who holds the key for today,
Who has countless times opened doors and made you a way,
And renewed your hope in the new dawning day,
When in doubt, shout Hallelujah, Jesus is mine!

When the blessings in life flow full to overflowing
There are so many coming from directions unknown,
Remember that Jesus does now and forever will,
Answer the prayers of His children when they call,
He will never let His loved ones fall.
If you just pray and wait, for His time is never too late.
You can call Him any time of the day and of the night,
When in doubt, shout Hallelujah, Jesus is mine!

WHEN IT IS YOUR TURN

When it's time for you to account
For all the things you have done in life
Wrong or right, you choose the path to take,
Will you stand tall and confess,
Or hang your head in shame,
When it is your turn to stand before the King?

You knew the time was coming soon,
And one day you would be called upon,
Wrong or right, you choose the path you took,
Will you stand as bold as when,
You made that choice to sin,
When it is your turn to stand before the King?

Will you bow before King Jesus,
And ask for forgiveness for all your sins,
You know He will forgive without a doubt.
You and He are the only ones who will stand there,
No one else will see,
When it is your turn to stand before the King?

Did you ever ask for forgiveness,
For the wrongs done in your life
Ever get down on your knees and cry
Lord, please have mercy on me,
For I am not worthy, you see,
I am not worthy of standing before your throne.

What will you do when it is your turn to stand before the King?
What will you do when it is your turn to stand before the King?

ALL SHALL PRAISE HIS NAME

All that hear His voice,
Shall praise His name.
All the know His powerful works,
Shall spread the word.
All who believe can readily perceive,
And all shall praise His name.

The winds shall carry His word,
Across the vast universe.
All who know His powerful works,
And share a joyous state.
All who believe can readily perceive,
And all shall praise His name.

I KNOW THAT GOD SAVED ME

Nevertheless, he saved them for his name's sake, that he might make his mighty power to be known.

PSALMS 106:8

SMILES

Smiles are like flowers the bloom every day,
Sunshine that brightens our paths in every way
Smile for today, for tomorrow's not promised
Let the flowers grow, they brighten our lives
More than you know.

HE IS SO GOOD

The Lord has been so good to me
He has opened doors I could not see
I am weak and He is strong
But by His love I can go on.

The Lord, My God, to me is real
No one else I know can make sweet peace.
I dare not leave from this great love,
It cannot be replaced when lost or wronged.

YOUR LIGHT

You have got to let your light shine
So, all the world can see.

A vital force, a peaceful being
A guiding scintilla, all can see.

And maybe the light in you
That shines so gloriously each day.

Will awaken someone else's sleeping soul
To the light of love today.

WHISPERING IN THE WIND

Jesus is calling you, sit down and listen
Hear what He has to say
Jesus is calling you, sit still and hear
What words He has for you.
Sit down and listen to the Lord
Before the whisper turns into a roar.

Things may not be as tough as you think
You know they can be worse.
Your clothes aren't new, kids need shoes
Bills are due, you suffer the working man's or woman's blues.
But - Jesus has His hand on you
As He guides you every day
Just pray for a better way.

Jesus is calling you
And you keep walking away
You wander around like Jonah
Always going the opposite way.
The Lord sends you to the left and you turn right.
The lord sends you North, you go South.

You continue going in the wrong direction
Turn around, sit down, be still, listen
Sit down and listen to the Lord
Before the whisper turns into a roar.

Chorus
He is only whispering in the wind
The message He wants you to hear
Sit down and listen to the Lord
Before the whisper turns into a roar.

HALLELUJAH, JESUS SET ME FREE

There is no secret what God can do
What He's done for others
He will do for you.

Just trust and believe in Him
He will bring you through
There's no limit to what God can do.

I remember the blind man who was made to see
Jesus said Don't tell the world, just be quiet and let them see
The man was so happy, he shouted out loud
Hallelujah, Jesus is the man who brought me round.

The Israelites cried when they reached the Red Sea
Tired and driven they faltered in their belief
But God's Hand moved, and the sea parted
A Highway to Heaven up the road they started.

There was time when I didn't understand
That to make it through life I had to hold onto Jesus's Hand
But thank God for the change in me and now I see,
Hallelujah, Jesus' love set me free!

There was a sick lady who wanted to be made whole
She just reached out and touched the hem of Jesus' robe
And the Power within became the Power without
Have Mercy Jesus, how that lady did shout.

Hallelujah Jesus set me free (3)
He set me free on Calvary
Thank God for the change in me
Hallelujah, Jesus' love set me free.

THE CASTLE

I want the Lord to take me up
To that castle in the sky
To live forever in the glorious light.
I will wear a robe that is snow white
And walk the streets of gold
Never ever will the love of Jesus grow old.

When He comes for me, I plan to be ready
I have been preparing for a long, long time,
For the raptured day.
I will feel His glorious presence
In my life along the way
And I look toward the castle in the sky.

I KNOW THAT GOD SAVED ME

God reached out His hand to me
And said just a touch is all you need,
Just believe in me, I will set you free,
I know God saved me.

Many years ago, when I was sinking deep in sin
I found Jesus and was filled from deep within,
I knew all along that Jesus was there,
I was the one who didn't know where.

But one day something caused me to turn around
And Jesus love came in leaps and bounds,
He had opened many doors for me,
From my burdens and sorrows, He set me free,

My enemies no longer do me harm
Jesus my love, my life, my charm
I live now so that everyone can see
I know God saved me.

JESUS CARES
(TODAY HIS LOVE IS
THE ONLY WAY)

I want to spread the news
Jesus is coming back soon
Going to put on my walking shoes
And go and spread the news.
Jesus is coming back soon,
You better get ready.

Has everybody heard the news
Jesus Christ is coming back soon
I am going to put on my walking shoes
So, I can go and spread the news
Going to tell you what He has done for me
That is how I know He is the living Christ.

Going to tell everybody everywhere
Give yourself to Christ today
Don't you know He works miracles today
Those who know don't stray away
Let His grace and words fill your heart
And you have already made a good start.

CHORUS
Jesus cares today, His love is the only way
Jesus cares tonight, Jesus' love will show you right
Jesus loves right now
If you let Him show you how
Jesus loves us all
If you just heed His call.

I FOUND JESUS

I went to the river
It chilled me to the bone
I found I was yearning
For a warming in my soul.

I looked all around me
And a man I did see
I did not know who He was
However, He beckoned to me.

He took me by my hand
And led me to the water
He said, "do Not worry none,
Because what I have got is number one.

I found Jesus
I found Jesus
I found Jesus
And He made everything all right.

The water eased my body
And it warmed my soul
Before I knew it,
I had lost all control.

My feet they stomped
My hands they waved
To my new friend Jesus,
I was giving all the praise.

I found Jesus
I found Jesus
I found Jesus
And He made everything all right.

JUST A LITTLE FAITH

Just a little faith
Is all you need.

To see the wonders God wants you to see
To climb a mountain high
Or swim in the ocean deep.

To soar with eagles
Swim with the fishes in the deep

Just a little faith
Hallelujah! Is all you'll ever need!

You may tire of walking around in despair
You might never believe that anyone cares
But I know it - so I can share
Jesus will always be right there.

Hold your head up high and look around
God has got nothing for you low, down on the ground
Look upward toward the heavenly clouds
Just a little faith, Hallelujah! Is all you need!

THE FUTURE

The time has come to say good-bye
To my family and my friends
Now I must be moving on, to step out on my own.

I just want to say I love you
And thank you for all you have done
For soon I will begin a journey
That no one else can make for me.

I am stepping out of the familiar
And I am walking into the new
I would like to take your blessings with me,
And some of your prayers too.

Please hold me in your memories
And keep me in your heart
And know that God has a definite plan,
For all his children near and far.

GOD WILL NEVER LET YOU FALL

Deliver me, O Lord, from my enemies: I flee unto thee to hide me.

PSALM 143:9

GOD WILL NEVER LET YOU FALL

The climb is never easy
When you try to reach the top of the mountain.
The climb is never easy
When you stop and take that look back
From where you've come from.
It seems your troubles are catching up with you
They're gaining on every hand,
But it you keep your eye on the prize
And finish the climb
God will never let you fall.

He'll never let you fall,
Though it seems your burdens are too much to bear.
He'll never let you fall,
Just trust in Jesus and he'll be - right there.

If you keep your eye on the prize and finish the climb
God will never let you fall.

Steadfast, unmovable, always abounding in His word
They that wait on the Lord
Shall renew their strength
They shall mount up on wings like eagles
They shall walk and not get weary.

Yes, yes, yes, yes Lord
Keep your eye on the prize and finish the climb
God will never let you fall.

JESUS POWER

There are times when troubles just seem to block my path,
There are times when worries crease my suffering brow
There are times when burdens get heavy.
And midnight never seems to end.

There are problems that have no solution
There are puzzles that never get solved
There are trials that we seem to have
And the answers just cannot be found.

But you can call Him up, every night or day
You can call Him up anytime, you can call Him anywhere
Just call His name, call His Name, Call His name out loud.

I'm talking about
Jesus, Jesus, Jesus, Oh Jesus
Jesus, Jesus, Jesus, Sweet Jesus
Call His name, call His name, call His name out loud.

He's the answer to all your problems
He's the solution to every puzzle
If you just kneel and pray
The Savior will show you the way.

He's the way when days are dreary
And the midnights never seem to end,
He's the way out of darkness
And into the marvelous light.

CHORUS
I call
Jesus, Jesus, Jesus, Oh Jesus
Jesus, Jesus, Jesus, Sweet Jesus
Call His name, call His name, call His name out loud.

You know all you need is some Jesus Power
He'll come through every time
When the road gets rough and the going gets tough
He's the answer that can always be found.

LEADER
He will pick you up
Turn you around
Place your feet right back
On solid ground.
You just call His name, call His name, call His name out loud.

CHORUS
I call
Jesus, Jesus, Jesus, Oh Jesus, Jesus, Jesus, Jesus, Sweet Jesus
Call His name, call His name,
You just call His name out loud.

Lyrics Karolyn Jennings, Musical Arrangement Beverly Hynson

LOOK UP

What a beautiful day this is
God made it just for you
What a glorious day I see
Wake up before it no longer be.

God holds it all in His mighty hand
Entwined and bound with love
How can you live through this glorious day
If you sleep, it all away.

Open your eyes to the sunshine
God made it just for you.
He made the mountains and valleys
Too great a job for man to do.

He gave you wisdom and knowledge
Grace that would see you through
He made you able to reason
Something He knew you should be able to do.

So, walk each day in His sunshine
Trust and He will take your hand
Give love from your heart to every man
And God will love you in return.

A FAITHFUL PRAYER

Every now and then, the devil will step in
Encasing you with sin
Then the Lord will take your hand
So, His child can have a chance
He won't let you cry long in vain
Although your cry seems long and strained.

The world is in turmoil everywhere
But don't fret the Lord does care
Trust in Him no matter what you see
Things you see aren't always as they should be.
Don't let your faith forsake you in danger
Although you scream and cry out in anger.

He is always there to be your friend
So, take the hard times and the good times
The happy and the sad times
Give them all to the Lord who cares
All your trouble He will certainly share
The Lord always hears a faithful prayer.

MIGHTY IS THE LORD

Jesus is so mighty
He has got legions at His hand
He has set His word in motion
It is time to understand.

He has unleashed His mighty angels
Into a world full of sin
They are fighting by the hundreds of thousands
In a battle He will win.

Time is out for standing around
And saying that is not my concern
Time is out for turning your head the other way
And saying not today!

You have forgotten whose child you are
You have forgotten who set you free
Jesus is sending a wake-up call
It is up to you and me.

CHORUS
We are not made to have all the power
God's fate we cannot override
And we may not understand
We are just a pawn in God's army
Led by Jesus, He is the man.
He is the man of every hour
He is the man with all the power.
He is the mighty, mighty Prince of Peace,
Only He can set you free.

MARVEL

Somedays I sit and marvel, at just how far I have come
I am grateful for each loving day, and glad to see each morning sun.

I think of where I had plans to go
And of all the other places I have been,
And I still have years ahead of me
To make each journey begin.

I am no longer in my teens, but still young enough to dream
I am no longer waiting for the future; my future begins with each new day.

So do not think that tomorrow
When your hair has turned gray
There is nothing left to reach for
Death is not a step away.

Sit back and marvel at how far you have come
And let your future begin, again, with each morning sun.

What is life?
Without a goal to reach.
What is life?
Without a song to sing.

And yes!
My journey has just begun.

CARRY ON IN THE NAME OF THE LORD

No matter the trials of time
Or the temptations that abide
Whatever may be, Jesus has the last decree.

No matter if friends put you down
And no one wants you around
Whatever may be, Jesus is the friend you need.

The road of life is not straight and narrow
Neither free from heartache nor sorrow
Whatever may be, Jesus is the one for me.

Lord, I know you lifted me
Lord, I know you comforted me
And now I am able, I will carry on in the name of the Lord.

CHORUS

Carry on in the name of the Lord
No matter what the outcome
He is all the help you need
When men will try and use you
Whatever may be, Jesus is the only one you need.

YOU WILL FIND ALL YOU NEED IN ME

I am meek and lowly
Humble, wise and Holy
I am the Alpha and the Omega
You will find all you need in Me.

I am He who walks on water
I am the Sun that shines from sea to sea
I am the Beginning and the Ending,
You will find All you need in Me.

Some people call me Jesus
The Rose of Sharon, The Lily of the Valley
Emmanuel and the Great Prince of Peace
They call me, He Who Always Listens,
You will find all you need in Me.

VERSE

When you have searched from shore to shore
You still don't know what you are looking for
You can travel from sea to sea
And fly the heavens beyond man's reach.

When bright lights have slowly dimmed
The games of life you no longer win
When you have searched everywhere you can
And you still cannot find or understand.

Just stand still and I will hear your plea
You will find all you need in Me.

AND WHY SHOULD I BE AFRAID

Though men may plot and scheme
Against me and all I believe,
Though men may try to find my
weakness and hurt me in the end.

Though I may falter along the way
and sometimes feel alone,
I know the Lord is standing by
to lift me when I fall.

I know the Lord will answer prayer
and cause miracles to unfold,
He will take my enemies, and make them friends
and heal my wounded soul.

And why should I be afraid
When friends forsake me
If someone seeks my downfall
I have the Lord on my side
Forever there to abide.

And why should I be afraid
If the world cannot understand
The significance of His plans
That my heart has been blessed
With His righteousness
And
My mind is made up
To live for the Lord.

THE DEVIL IS WORKING OVERTIME

The devil is working overtime, he is coming after you
He wants to take control of your soul, and work his will with you,
The devil is working overtime, when he hears you pray.
He likes to interfere when you call on God each day.
But one thing that you will know, no matter what you do,
You are still a child of God, and He will take care of you.

The devil is working overtime, trying to win your soul
Do not worry that he is somewhere else, he is also watching you.
He is watching and he is waiting near, for your next mistake
He is slinking and he is creeping, because he is just a snake.
You better work it out with God, because no matter what you do
The devil is working overtime, and he is coming after you.

The devil is working overtime when you are not, he watches you each day
When you are weak and weary, and you forget to pray.
He is waiting there to call your name, to catch you unaware,
Calling you seductively to do his work today.
So, listen when you hear a voice, a voice that calls to you
Just be aware, call God instead and He will see you through.

The devil is working overtime, he is coming after you.
You do not dare let your guard down, that would be a big mistake.
Get back, get back
Get down, get out
Devil you are not welcome here.

Get back, get back
Get down, get out
Devil you are not welcome here.

Do not let the devil ruin your day
Work it out with God,

Get back, get back
Get down, get out
Devil you are not welcome here.

Get back, get back
Get down, get out
Devil you are not welcome here.

HEAVEN BOUND

*And when he had opened the seventh seal,
there was silence in heaven
about the space of half an hour.*

REVELATION 8:1

I'M GOING HOME TODAY

The sun and moon and stars above
A world of wonder that I adore and
The love of my family.
All of this I leave behind
I am going home today.
God touched my body
And called my name
I heard Him say to me
You have spent enough time
Upon the earth,
Today you come with me.
So, weep for me
And then rejoice
For I go to a heavenly place
O' say goodbye to all that I love,
I am going home today.

HOMEWARD BOUND

When God calls His saints home
On earth no longer to abide.
When He has decided they are no longer for loan
Forever in heaven they will abide.
When the saints of God return
At life's end to forever reside
Within heaven's gates.
However soon it will be,
I do not want the Lord to forget me
Then I too, will be homeward bound.

I HEARD JESUS CALL

You know I heard Jesus' call to me
I heard Him call my name
He called so sweet
His voice was low and clear.
You know I heard Jesus call my name
Oh yes, Jesus called to me.

REMEMBER

Time is symbolized in the changing of the seasons
God moves His hands on our lives for various reasons,
Love blossoms and grows as each new life is born,
And escalates in proportion as the years wear on.
We live fully and love fully until we depart this earth.
But memories last forever and God's love wins over all obstacles

CHRISTIAN WOMEN

Warm
Open-minded
Multi-talented
Ever-loving and everlasting,
Non-failing in God's work.

We walk the way of this world
But we walk not to this world
We work and strive for the best
Raise our families, maintain jobs just like the rest
We marry, bear children, we are blessed.

We walk the walk of Jesus Christ
We talk the talk he talked.
Temptations often rock our sturdy stand,
Trials come on every hand,
But Jesus' way is our steadfast plan.

Wife, mother, lover, and child
We are women unchanged by time,
The roles we live will never change
As we grow in grace and strength and faith.

We are Christian women
Walking onward
Non-stop in the name of Jesus Christ.
We grow in grace and strength and faith,
God's hand has touched us and shown us the way.

MOVE UP JUST A LITTLE BIT HIGHER

I am trusting in every way
Trusting on my faith that one day
Praying soon that day will come
And I'll move up to higher ground.

I have been working hard all my life
Doing the best I can and trusting God
I know soon that day will come
And I'll move up to higher ground.

Chorus
Move up just a little bit higher
Move up just a little bit higher
Move up just a little bit higher
Move up to higher ground.

Karolyn E. Jennings, Lyricist and Arranger

THAT DAY NOT SO FAR AWAY

One day I will see Jesus with His crown of gold
Wearing a robe so white, He is the Master of my Life.
One day I will see Jesus, hear His voice so sweet,
He will call my name, and my whole life will be complete.

Chorus

One day the trumpets will sound on high
And the dead in Christ will rise
That day, not so far away, I will hear my Jesus say
Come unto me my sweet, sweet child,
For your night is finally over
You have now come into the marvelous light.

It is time to rejoice in This Day
Say farewell to the world below and
Come rejoice with Me on high.

A HOMEGOING SONG

Every step of the way
Through each and every day,
And those many nights
Lord, I know you heard my cry.

You answered every prayer
Whispered or thought,
Lord God Almighty
Your love was surely wrought.

You molded me and made me
Into the person You wanted me to be,
I pray that those around me
Also saw the goodness You planted in me.

I was waiting for Your call
Though some may believe it came too soon,
But you know all, and You love all
The right time, you alone, only knew.

God granted me grace as I finished my long journey,
God granted me peace from the troubles of this world,
God granted many blessings throughout the life I leave behind,
I bid you farewell, and I will see you on the other side.

WHEN YOU STAND IN FRONT OF GOD
In Loving Memory of Rev. Frank Calloway

God will remember you for all the love you have shown others
The souls you have loved and,
The time you gave and,
Your struggle to live right
Every day of your life.

I'll recall your thundering sermons
From the Pulpit Sunday morn
And the comfort you gave to
Those who had to mourn.

For your strength and courage
To stand up to those who didn't believe,
That there is a God in heaven that we
Must one day perceive.

God grant you safe passage
A beautiful life beyond the tears and fears
Of earthly
bonds.

These poems were written from the sermons you preached over the years. Thank you for your inspiration.

JESUS SAVED ME

My defense is of God, which saveth the upright in heart.

PSALMS 7:10

WALKING WITH JESUS

My shoes are worn
My clothes aren't new
But my faith in Jesus
    Will see me through.

I have come this far
I cannot turn around
I know He will answer
    Me right on time.

I have been walking with Jesus
All of my life
He is always by my side,
    Whether I am wrong or right.

My faith keeps me near
I know He will hear
    Whenever I call,
        Whenever I call.

FAMILY AND FRIEND DAY

Mother call me up today, to say
This Sunday let us go home
To the church you joined when you were eight,
Has called us today to abide.

They will be singing, shouting and praying
This Sunday so you will know
The Lord is still alive and inspiring
And dwelling at Morning Star.

Maybe I will find something I lost
Maybe a little more faith
But if I do not go, I will never know
What blessing the day will impart.

So, I will be going home again
This Sunday, just look for me
As the Church I joined when I was eight,
Is still a home for me.

COME UNTO ME

Come unto me
    My sweet, sweet child
Come unto me and rest.
Dry your weeping eyes
    And smile (pray)
For I love you.

For I love you on this day.

Come unto me
    My sweet, sweet child
Come unto me and pray
I will fight your battles
    If you give them all away.

Just call me when you kneel and pray.

Come unto me
    My sweet, sweet child
Come unto me and rest.

When you learn patience to believe and trust
    You will be blessed,

LORD LINGER NEAR

When my day grows dark and drear
Linger near,
When my day goes from, up to down
Linger near,
When my daylight turns into a dark night
And I struggle to do what's right
Lord, I need you to linger near.

When my joy turns into sorrow
Linger near,
When my hope I cannot see
Linger near,
When my day turns into night
And I struggle to do what's right
Lord, I need you to linger near.

You are all that I need Lord
You are all that I need Lord.

Take my hand in times of trouble,
Take my heart in times of sorrow
I need you to linger near
You are all I need, Lord
You are all I need.

JESUS SET ME FREE

Jesus set me free
The day He died on Calvary
Jesus set me free
When He gave His life for me.

Jesus set me free
And I am so thankful that He did
He died for me, He set me free
Now I can live for Him.

I am so glad that Jesus died for me
I am so glad because no one else could set me free
He gave His life for me
And now I have been set free,
Now I can live my life and be free.

Lyrics and music by Karolyn Jennings

He that dwelleth in the secret place of the
most High shall abide under the
shadow of the Almighty.
He shall cover thee with his feathers, and
under His wings should thou
trust: His truth shall be thy shield and buckler.
───────────
PSALMS 91 VERSES1 AND 4

Milton Keynes UK
Ingram Content Group UK Ltd.
UKHW030913121124
451094UK00001B/90